Be Mindful!
Be Here Now

Bobbie Kalman

Crabtree Publishing Company
www.crabtreebooks.com

Be Your Best SElf
Building Social-Emotional Skills

Created by Bobbie Kalman

For Kathryn Richmond,
with much thanks to a wonderful friend
who introduced me to and taught me about Mindfulness

Author and Editor-in-Chief
Bobbie Kalman

Editor
Kathy Middleton

Proofreader
Crystal Sikkens

Photo research
Bobbie Kalman

Design
Bobbie Kalman
Katherine Berti
Samantha Crabtree
(text and cover)

Print and production coordinator
Katherine Berti

Special thanks to:
Darcy Patrick for his inspiration on Cloud Gazing on pages 14–15
Francine Jarry for the poem on page 7
Thich Nhat Hanh for inspiration of the poem on page 10

Images:
© iStockphoto.com: page 19 (bottom center); page 27 (top right)
© Shutterstock.com: Cover and all other photographs and images

Library and Archives Canada Cataloguing in Publication

Title: Be mindful! : be here now / Bobbie Kalman.
Names: Kalman, Bobbie, author.
Description: Series statement: Be your best self: building social-emotional skills
 | Includes index.
Identifiers: Canadiana (print) 20190134410 | Canadiana (ebook) 20190134429 |
 ISBN 9780778767060 (hardcover) |
 ISBN 9780778767107 (softcover) |
 ISBN 9781427124173 (HTML)
Subjects: LCSH: Mindfulness (Psychology)—Juvenile literature. | LCSH:
 Awareness—Juvenile literature. | LCSH: Conduct of life—Juvenile literature.
Classification: LCC BF637.M56 K35 2019 | DDC j158.1/3—dc23

Library of Congress Cataloging-in-Publication Data

Names: Kalman, Bobbie, author.
Title: Be mindful! : be here now / Bobbie Kalman.
Description: New York : Crabtree Publishing Company, [2020] |
 Series: Be your best self: building social-emotional skills | Includes index.
Identifiers: LCCN 2019023737 (print) | LCCN 2019023738 (ebook) |
 ISBN 9780778767060 (hardcover) | ISBN 9780778767107 (hardcover) |
 ISBN 9781427124173 (ebook)
Subjects: LCSH: Mindfulness (Psychology)--Juvenile literature.
Classification: LCC BF637.M56 K35 2020 (print) | LCC BF637.M56 (ebook) |
 DDC 155.4/1913--dc23
LC record available at https://lccn.loc.gov/2019023737
LC ebook record available at https://lccn.loc.gov/2019023738

Crabtree Publishing Company

www.crabtreebooks.com   1-800-387-7650

Printed in the U.S.A./102019/CG20190809

Published in Canada
Crabtree Publishing
616 Welland Ave.
St. Catharines, Ontario
L2M 5V6

Published in the United States
Crabtree Publishing
PMB 59051
350 Fifth Avenue, 59th Floor
New York, New York 10118

Published in the United Kingdom
Crabtree Publishing
Maritime House
Basin Road North, Hove
BN41 1WR

Published in Australia
Crabtree Publishing
Unit 3 – 5 Currumbin Court
Capalaba
QLD 4157

Contents

What is mindfulness?

Mindfulness is the practice of paying attention to what is happening around you at the moment with an attitude of kindness and curiosity. We often **focus**, or pay attention to, the things that worry us. Mindfulness is a way to shift our focus to positive thoughts instead of the things that worry us. When we make ourselves pay attention in the present moment, we begin to let go of our worries. Mindfulness helps us be more positive and less negative. It allows us to handle difficult emotions, so they don't control us. Mindfulness teaches us to be **aware** of how we feel and learn to let go of our negative feelings instead of fighting them.

The children below are drawing pictures and writing words about mindfulness. This book will show you ways that you can practice mindfulness to help you live in a kinder, more positive world.

Smile

Dream

just breathe

Relax

Play

Love

Mindfulness will help you:
- enjoy school and other activities more
- pay attention to what you are learning
- show more kindness to others
- be aware of what makes you happy
- be more grateful for your life
- learn to be your own best friend
- worry less and have more fun

Be here NOW!

When you are calm, your body is resting. Your breathing is slow, your muscles are relaxed, and your heart is beating normally. When you feel **anxious**, your heart beats faster, and it can be harder to breathe. You can change how you feel, however, by changing how you breathe.

Mindful breathing

Close your eyes and focus on your breathing. Inhale, or take in, a big breath of air through your nose while you count to four. Can you feel the air moving through your nose? With your hands on your belly, pull that air all the way in until you feel your hands rise on your belly. Hold the air in while you count to four. Then exhale, or push the air out through your nose, counting to four again. Does your breath feel warmer on its way out? How does your breath sound when you breathe in and out?

Fill your body with a happy breath.

When you exhale, breathe out any sad thoughts or feelings.

Happy breaths

Mindful breathing makes you focus on your breath so you do not think about anything else. It helps you be in the present—not the past or future. When you inhale, think of something that makes you feel happy. Fill your body with that happy breath. Then send that happy feeling out to the world. Your good wishes will travel with each breath you exhale.

Quiet time

When you spend time being quiet, your mind becomes clearer. You feel happier and more in touch with the real you. You become confident and feel more powerful and less afraid. You think of life as a gift. To keep your mind on good thoughts, repeat the statements below or ones that you have made up.

- I am good.
- I am **unique**. There is no one like me.
- I am happy to be me.
- I love myself and others.

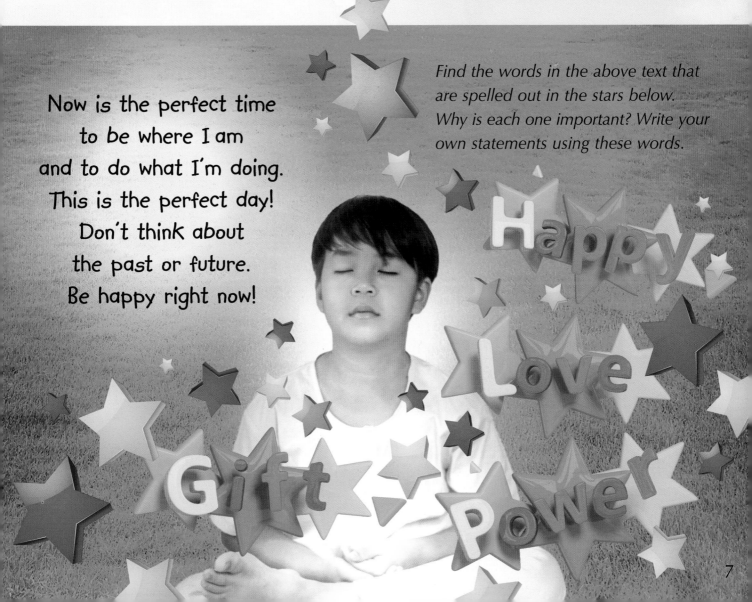

Now is the perfect time to be where I am and to do what I'm doing. This is the perfect day! Don't think about the past or future. Be happy right now!

Find the words in the above text that are spelled out in the stars below. Why is each one important? Write your own statements using these words.

Happy
Love
Gift
Power

Fun ways to breathe

One of the best ways to remember to breathe all the way into your belly is to use a breathing buddy, or stuffed animal. Place it against your belly as you sit or lie down on your back. As you breathe in and out, your buddy should be moving up and down. Breathing like this helps you learn to use your belly to take big, deep breaths. It's okay if your mind starts to wander. Your breathing buddy will help bring your attention back to the present.

Breathing Buddy

Circle Breathers

These kids are breathing together. Their arms go up when they breathe in and down when they breathe out.

You can learn other fun ways to breathe on these pages. Try them and see which are your favorites.

Bubble Breath

Pinwheel Breath

Using deep breaths, blow bubbles carefully and slowly. As you count to four, breathe in, hold your breath, and exhale through your mouth. Blow the bubbles as you exhale. How many counts did it take to blow the bubbles with the breath you exhaled?

Use a pinwheel to breathe. Make the pinwheel spin as you exhale.

Bunny Breath

Make "bunny paws" in front of your chest and take quick sniffs like a bunny. While taking quick breaths, hop like a bunny.

sniff
sniff
breathe

hop
hop
breathe

Bumblebee Breath

Breathe in and pretend you are a bumblebee smelling a flower. As you breathe out, make a humming bee sound. Try making the sound longer or shorter, higher or lower.

Good morning, Sun

Another morning is here. Breathing in,
I wake my body. Breathing out, I smile.
Opening the window, I look out and see
my world covered in sunlight. How
wonderful life is! I am happy to be alive!
I look in the mirror and see myself.
My mind and heart are open to love.

Breathing in,
my breath goes deep.
Breathing out,
my breath goes slow.
Breathing in makes me calm.
Breathing out makes me happy.
With each in-breath, I smile.
With each out-breath, I let go.
When I breathe in,
I am in the present moment.
When I breathe out,
I feel it is
a wonderful moment!

When I turn on the water to wash my face, I remember that my body is more than 70% water. Without water, I would have no food, nothing to drink, and no baths!

When I look in the mirror, I smile with my eyes, as well as my lips. I am mindful of who I am. I am grateful for my clothes and my healthy body. I can't wait to play soccer today!

When I eat breakfast, I am thankful for the air, water, and sunlight that made it possible to grow the foods I eat. I am also grateful for being able to share my meals with my wonderful family.

Mindfulness meditation

Meditation is an activity that helps us slow down our busy minds and bodies so we can be present in the moment. Meditation helps us calm our nerves and reduce any **anxiety**, or worries, that we are feeling. It gives us time to become quiet and learn to ignore some of the things that are causing us to worry. Meditation gives our minds a break. It is like a mini-vacation for our brains. Meditation encourages us to pay attention to the present. It makes us live in the moment instead of worrying about the past or being anxious about the future. We can't change what happened in the past and we can't predict the future. We can only control the present. Meditation helps us be here now.

During mindful meditation, your breathing and heartbeat will slow down.

How to meditate

- Sit comfortably with your legs crossed, or lie down. It is important to sit up straight or lie straight on your back.

    - Start breathing in and out as naturally as possible and focus your attention on your breath, feeling your belly rise and fall.

    - If you find your mind drifting, or thoughts start popping into your head, gently bring yourself back to noticing your breathing again.

Meditating in school will help you pay attention and learn more easily.

"Talking" thoughts

While meditating, thoughts may often float into your head and talk to you. What emotions do they tell you that you are feeling?

Are you angry, worried, or afraid?

Are you tense? Do you have any pain?

Are you calm, happy, or loving?

Where do you feel these emotions in your body?

5 senses

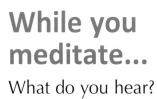

While you meditate...

What do you hear?

What do you see?

What do you taste?

What do you smell?

What do you feel?

Cloud gazing

Cloud gazing is an activity that gives us a different way of looking at our thoughts. Like clouds, our thoughts are always forming, changing, and moving on. Gazing at clouds allows us to see our thoughts as something that we can keep or allow to just float away.

How would it feel to be high up in the sky? How do you think clouds feel? Are they like huge cotton balls or fluffy cool air? What if you were a superhero who could fly up into these puffy formations and be free of any negative thoughts or emotions?

Take some deep breaths

Spend a few moments just looking at the clouds. See them dance, float, and change shapes on their journey across the sky. Does it feel like you're dreaming? Start your cloud adventure by taking a few deep breaths. As you breathe, relax each body part and allow your muscles to soften and let go. Feel yourself becoming lighter and lighter as you begin to float slowly—up, up, up, into the sky. Feel your body become weightless. The world below you is not there now because only flying is on your mind.

Daydream your best life

Daydreaming takes us away to a fantasy world that makes us feel happy. Flying in the sky is a perfect way to daydream. Fly above the clouds and create your best world. Think of how you can make your dream world real when you are back on the ground.

Watch the clouds move slowly across the sky.
Change them into beautiful daydreams.

Mindful yoga

Mindful yoga is a combination of yoga and mindfulness. Mindfulness is training yourself to focus on what is happening now. Yoga is an exercise made up of poses called **asanas**. Asanas make your body stronger by stretching your muscles. Mindful yoga helps you build balance, strength, and focus. Yoga can also help reduce **stress**. Be curious and open to what you are noticing while you are doing yoga. Look at the poses on these pages. Which ones would you like to do? Do them very carefully and be gentle on yourself.

*The girl above is doing a **Lotus Pose**. It is named after the lotus flower, shown behind her. This pose is often used during meditation. The legs are crossed, and the index finger and thumb on each hand are touching.*

*The **Camel Pose** gives you the courage to face your problems. You need to keep your balance while you bend backwards to grab your ankles. Can you do this pose? Does it make you feel brave?*

*The **Cobra Pose** stretches your chest and helps you deal with stress. It also makes you feel less tired.*

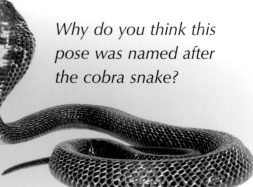

Why do you think this pose was named after the cobra snake?

The **Downward Dog Pose** is a forward bend that looks like a dog stretching.

The **Tree Pose** helps you learn to stay balanced and be more patient.

The **Child Pose** is a resting pose. It calms you down and helps you be more mindful of your breath. Do it from one to three minutes.

How long can you hold this pose? Do you feel balanced in your body and mind?

The **Corpse Pose** is the last pose at the end of a yoga session.

The **Crow Pose** helps your mind focus and improves your balance.

It is a thank you to your body for all the work it has done.

17

The children above are walking through a forest in autumn. Name three things they might see, hear, touch, and smell as they walk.

Sensing nature

We all share the same home—Earth. Earth is the only planet that has air, water, and food. Only Earth has plants, animals, and people. We are all part of nature. No matter where we live, we depend on nature. No machine can make oxygen as well as a tree can, nor can people make food using sunlight, the way plants do. We can become more mindful of nature by taking walks and using our five senses—sight, sound, smell, taste, and touch—while we walk.

Some of the children are lying on top of the fallen leaves. How do leaves look and feel?

How does this boy show his gratitude to nature?

What is he seeing and feeling above his head and below his feet?

How does it feel to walk on sand at the beach? How is it different from walking in water?

A mindful nature walk

Before beginning your nature walk, take three or more deep breaths.

- As you walk, notice how your body feels. If you are walking barefoot, how does the ground feel under your feet? How do your legs, feet, and arms feel with each step you take?
- Using your sense of sight, look around and pay attention to every detail. Are there things you can touch, such as leaves, tree trunks, or flowers? Describe how each thing feels.
- Using your sense of smell, notice any **aromas**, or scents, in the air. Describe what you smell.
- Are you eating a snack you brought with you? How does it taste?
- Before you end your walk, check in on your breath, notice your feet, and think about how your mind and body are feeling. What stands out the most about your walk?

To be even more mindful of nature, you can volunteer to plant some trees or pick up trash in your community.

19

Healthy body, healthy mind

Just by breathing, the body is performing magic every moment—it is keeping you alive! It keeps you growing, moving, and feeling. Practicing mindfulness makes you feel happy to be alive! The body is always in the present. You can only feel right now—not yesterday or tomorrow. You can learn how your entire body feels by doing a body scan. During a scan, you pay attention to each body part one at a time, becoming aware of how each feels.

Doing a body scan

Find a comfortable place on which to sit up or lie down. You can close your eyes or leave them open. Notice how your **posture**, or position of your body, feels. Pay attention to your toes for 5 to 10 seconds. Move on to your ankles, calves, knees, back, stomach, hands, arms, shoulders, neck, throat, jaw, face, ears, and the top of your head. As you focus on each body part, ask yourself these questions:

- How does this body part feel?
- Is it cold or warm?
- Does it feel tight or relaxed?
- What is touching this part? Is it clothing, the floor, or part of the furniture?
- What does that feel like?

How each body part feels brings awareness to your body in the moment. If there is tightness or stress, imagine breathing the stress out of that part of the body each time you exhale.

Helpful activities

A body scan will help make you aware of what is happening in your body and mind. This page shows other things you can do to help keep your body and mind healthy. Keep a journal of what you are doing each day to keep yourself healthy and happy.

Eat foods that are good for your body.

Get plenty of exercise, such as yoga, which stretches and relaxes your body. Mindful breathing and meditating are also very important for your body and mind.

Drink 6 to 8 glasses of water each day.

Spend time with friends. Laugh, play, and share your stories.

Get at least 10 hours of sleep every night.

Spend time outdoors as often as possible. Walk, ride your bike, swim, or play sports.

Eating mindfully

Eating should be one of our most enjoyable activities each day, but we tend to rush through our meals. Mindful eating encourages us to slow down and use our senses to make our meals taste even better. Take a moment before eating to notice the aroma, appearance, and **texture** of the food you are about to eat. Be mindful of how you lift the hand, fork, or spoon you are using to eat your food. When the food is in your mouth, pay close attention to each flavor and notice how the food feels, smells, and tastes as you eat it. When thoughts or feelings pop into your head, simply notice them and allow them to pass like clouds. Then bring your focus back to eating.

Describe how a raisin looks, feels, smells, and tastes.

The boy below is holding some oranges. How does an orange look and feel? What will he have to do before he eats one? When you peel an orange, describe the feel of the peel against your fingers. After peeling it, how does the fruit of the orange smell and taste?

Mindful eating practice

Choose a raisin for your first eating practice. How does it feel to touch it? Describe its texture. Now, close your eyes and hold the raisin in your mouth for 2 minutes without chewing it. How does it feel against your tongue and the roof of your mouth? How does it taste? Next, chew the raisin for 30 seconds. Does it taste different when you chew it than when you just held it in your mouth? How does it feel going down your throat and into your stomach?

Eating tips

- Give thanks for your food. Think of all the ingredients it contains and what it took for you to have it as a meal.
- Use your five senses to enjoy your food more.
- Eat more slowly.
- Eat in silence.
- Chew each mouthful of food 20 times.
- Take a breathing break after a few bites.
- Switch hands. Using your other hand will make your brain work harder.
- Stop eating after you are full.

This boy is eating ice cream. How does it feel against his lips, tongue, and teeth? If he eats it slowly, how will the feel and taste of the ice cream be different?

Create works of art to make your food even more interesting and fun to eat. You will enjoy looking at your art as well as touching, smelling, tasting, and listening to the crunchy sounds it makes. You may also hear compliments for your food art.

This girl is looking, touching, and smelling her pizza before she tastes it. How do you think it feels against her hands? Does the crust look hard or soft? Is the crust warm or hot? How can you tell?

Calming negative emotions

Go to a quiet place to calm down. A mindful walk in nature is an excellent way to clear your mind of negative thoughts. Breathe out your negative feelings and breathe in peaceful thoughts as you smell the beautiful flowers on your walk.

We have many kinds of emotions. Some make us feel happy, others make us sad, and some frighten us. Emotions come and go, just like clouds. We can have several kinds of emotions in a day. Positive emotions make us feel good. Negative emotions can make us feel unhappy, but they can also help us deal with challenges. Fear makes us aware of dangers or risks we might be taking. Sadness helps us connect with people who love us or can help protect us. **Resilience** helps us **adapt**, or adjust to, our negative emotions and quickly recover when we are stressed. The examples on these pages show ways that you can calm yourself when you feel sad, anxious, or angry. Don't forget meditation and yoga! Both will help calm you.

Lift some weights and do some stretches.

Read a book to take your mind off your problems.

Listen to music, sing, and dance! Nothing can change your mood as quickly as music can.

Look at some pictures that remind you of happy family times.

Take your dog for a long walk.

Write about your feelings and draw some pictures. Talk to an adult about what upset you.

Take a break, drink some water, and think of what would make you feel good. Be positive!

If you and a friend are angry with each other, share your feelings and then give each other a hug.

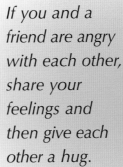

Be your own best friend!

The **authentic**, or real, you is the one that allows you to love and accept yourself just the way you are. It is the you that also loves others and looks at life in a joyful way. You are your authentic self when you are happy with yourself and the world around you. If you know what makes you feel happy or sad, you can do something about it.

I am creative.
I have great ideas.

I am positive.
I believe in myself.

Listen with your heart

You may not feel happy every day, but you can help yourself feel better. Take some deep, mindful breaths and listen to what your heart is telling you. Whatever your feelings are, they matter. Life is not perfect, but each challenge you have helps you become more resilient. Learning how to let go of your fear and adapt to change can make you stronger. You will become mindful of what brings you peace.

I listen with my heart when my friends share their challenges with me.

I am resilient and positive!

I am honest. I am kind. I am strong.
I am grateful for who I am
and everything I have.
I focus on my successes.
I have a good attitude.
I am not afraid to make mistakes.
I enjoy doing the things I love.
I love trying new things.
Each day I repeat three positive
statements that make me feel good.
I have fun with my friends.

My friends and I love the same music, we play sports together, and support one another in many ways.

As my own best friend, I accept myself with no exceptions. I face my challenges with confidence, not fear. I am good at solving problems.

Creating art makes me mindful of how I can communicate in different ways. It helps me calm down and be in the present moment.

Connected in life's journey

If you are happy, you will make others happy, too. We are not alone. Each one of us can make a difference to those around us. Our purpose in life is to learn about ourselves and others. When we believe in ourselves, we believe in others, too. We are all connected. How can you be a better friend? Becoming aware of the feelings of others is very important. We get strength from our connections. We can work together to create a world with more **empathy** and more heart.

Connect with friends who enjoy doing the things that are important to you. Are you into music, sports, yoga, volunteering, or pets? Find friends who love the same things.

Get together with some friends and share your stories about:
- what makes you happy
- your best and worst memories
- what you value most in a friend
- how you are the same and different from your friends
- your biggest success story so far
- how you can make the world a better place

A kinder, more positive world

Practicing mindfulness helps us in many ways. Our bodies and minds will notice a big difference. Mindfulness also helps create a kinder, more positive world. Being mindful of our decisions and choices creates better lives for ourselves and others. Are love, kindness, and gratitude part of who you are? How many mindful things do you do each day to make the world a better place?

*These children are pointing to the parts of the world from which their families have come. When people move from one country to another, they bring their **culture**, or way of life, with them. It is fun to learn about the cultures of others. Name three ways your culture is different from the cultures of some of your friends.*

A better life for all

The **common good** is the best possible life for everyone on Earth. We can help change the world by working for the common good in our family, school, and community. No matter what challenges life has given us, there is always someone who can use our help. Making a difference in the lives of others can make a huge difference in our lives, too! People remember us for the way we have treated others. How will people remember you?

How can we help?

Respect: We can respect others and be **inclusive** of them, even if we do not share their beliefs or cultures.

Kindness: We can show kindness by smiling, being friendly, giving compliments, and helping others.

United and connected: When we work as a team, we are united and feel connected. We can do anything!

Gratitude: Gratitude makes us happy because we realize how good our lives are. When we thank others, they feel happy, too. Happiness spreads quickly.

Glossary

Note: Some boldfaced words are defined where they appear in the book.

adapt To adjust to something new

anxiety A feeling of being worried

anxious Worried or nervous

aromas Pleasant scents or smells

asanas Yoga poses

authentic Real or genuine

aware Well-informed

common good The benefits of all people

culture Way of life, including customs and beliefs

empathy The ability to understand and share the emotions or feelings of others

focus To pay attention to something

inclusive Including all others

meditation The practice of focusing one's mind on relaxation

mindfulness A practice of being in the present moment and quieting your mind

posture The position in which a person holds his/her body when sitting or standing

resilience The ability to recover quickly from difficulties or negative emotions

stress The state of tension or mental strain during difficult times

texture The feel of an object's surface

unique One of a kind

Index